BATTLE
OF THE
BUTTS

BATTLE ★ OF THE ★ BUTTS

THE SCIENCE BEHIND ANIMAL BEHINDS

Written by
JOCELYN RISH

Illustrated by
DAVID CREIGHTON-PESTER

RP|KIDS
PHILADELPHIA

To Joyce, Robert, Brian, and Joanna:
the fanny-tastic family that always has my back . . . side.
—J.R.

For Laurelle, Joel, and Eloise
—D.C.

Running Press Kids
Hachette Book Group
1290 Avenue of the Americas, New York, NY 10104
www.runningpress.com/rpkids
@RP_Kids

Printed in China

First Edition: September 2021

Published by Running Press Kids, an imprint of Perseus Books, LLC, a subsidiary of Hachette Book Group, Inc.
The Running Press Kids name and logo is a trademark of the Hachette Book Group.

The Hachette Speakers Bureau provides a wide range of authors for speaking events. To find out more,
go to www.hachettespeakersbureau.com or call (866) 376-6591.

The publisher is not responsible for websites (or their content) that are not owned by the publisher.

Print book cover and interior design by Frances J. Soo Ping Chow

Library of Congress Control Number: 2019955706

ISBNs: 978-0-7624-9777-5 (hardcover), 978-0-7624-9778-2 (ebook),
978-0-7624-9862-8 (ebook), 978-0-7624-9863-5 (ebook)

APS

10 9 8 7 6 5 4 3 2 1

WELCOME TO THE BATTLE OF THE BUTTS!

Butts are funny. But they're also useful.
In fact, you're probably sitting on yours right now.

Humans use their butts for two primary functions—sitting and pooping. It's the same
for most other animals. However, some species have adapted to use their backsides in a number of surprising ways.
Some animals use their butts to protect themselves. Others build things with their butts.
A few even breathe through their butts!

With rear ends being used for all kinds of unusual things, the question is:
who has the best buttocks of them all?

That's for you to decide because you're the judge in the Battle of the Butts.

As you meet each challenger in this battle and learn about their **posterior** power,
it's up to you to rate them:

| 😎 TERRIFIC TUSHIE | 😀 REMARKABLE RUMP | 😎 COOL CABOOSE | 😕 PASSABLE POSTERIOR | 😣 BORING BACKSIDE |

You can assign your rating based on whatever factors you think are most important.
Maybe it's the strength of the posterior power. Or the weirdness of the posterior power.
Or even how much the posterior power makes you laugh. It's up to you!

Once you've judged them all, you will then crown the ultimate King of Keisters.

LET THE BATTLE OF THE BUTTS BEGIN!

CHALLENGER

1

THE PUDGY POOTER

INTRODUCING

THE MANATEE!

Genus: *Trichechus*

Length: 8 to 13 feet (2.4 to 4 meters)

Weight: 440 to 1,300 pounds (200 to 590 kilograms)

Home Turf: The warm tropical and subtropical coastal waters and rivers of eastern North and South America and western Africa

Posterior Power: They swim using farts.

Bluuurp! When you fart, you probably feel a sense of relief as the gas inside you escapes. For manatees, this release of gas is important because it helps them move up and down through the water. When they want to go up toward the surface, they hold in their farts. When they want to sink down, they let one rip!

Are you now picturing a manatee zipping through the water like it has a jetpack on its back end? That would be awesome. But it's actually a very slow motion, as the passing of gas changes their **buoyancy**. If you're thinking about trying to fart-swim the next time you're in the water, sadly, it won't work for humans. Manatees have special adaptations that have given them mega farts.

First of all, they eat a lot of plants. A whole lot of plants. You know how eating some veggies—like cauliflower, broccoli, and beans—will give you a serious case of the toots? Well, manatees eat for 6 to 8 hours a day chowing down on 60 to 200 pounds of water grasses, mangrove leaves, and algae. That's 10 percent of their body weight! Digesting all that vegetation creates a large supply of gas, giving them plenty of fuel for farting.

Manatees need to store all of this gas so they can control their buoyancy. Fortunately, their large intestines are *huge*. They can be up to 65 feet long and 6 inches in diameter, which is as long as a bowling lane and as wide as a dollar bill. That's a lot of guts filled with gas!

Extra Booty: Your large intestine is 5 feet long and 3 inches in diameter. If this were a battle of the large intestines, the manatee would totally blow you out of the water.

Manatees also have unusual **diaphragms**—they are longer and more powerful than other mammals. These super diaphragms help push gas around their bodies. Move the gas closer to the front end, and the manatee rises. Move the gas to its hind end so it fizzles out in a trail of bubbles, and the manatee sinks.

Butt Bonus:

WHEN MANATEES ARE UNABLE TO POOP BECAUSE THEY'RE CONSTIPATED, THEY LOSE BUOYANCY CONTROL AND FLOAT WITH THEIR TAILS HIGHER THAN THE REST OF THEIR BODIES. ONCE THEY ARE FINALLY ABLE TO POOP AGAIN, THEY WILL LET OUT A MASSIVE FART AND ARE THEN ABLE TO SWIM NORMALLY.

What do you think about being able to float using farts? How would you rate the manatee in the Battle of the Butts?

😃 TERRIFIC TUSHIE 😀 REMARKABLE RUMP 😎 COOL CABOOSE 😶 PASSABLE POSTERIOR 🙁 BORING BACKSIDE

CHALLENGER

2

THE TOUGH TUSHIE

INTRODUCING

THE WOMBAT!

Family: *Vombatidae*

Length: 28 to 47 inches (71 to 119 centimeters)

Weight: 32 to 80 pounds (14.5 to 36 kilograms)

Home Turf: The forests and grasslands of Australia

Posterior Power: Their butts are shields.

Wombats are **marsupials**, and like their kangaroo and koala cousins, they look like cuddly goofballs. But wombats are more like medieval knights, using their butts as shields to protect themselves and destroy their enemies.

Wombats are expert diggers; they create burrows and tunnels to live underground. At night, they venture out to eat. If they happen to run into a predator, like a dingo or a Tasmanian devil, they will run toward their burrow. Luckily, they're faster than they look. Their stumpy legs can reach 25 miles per hour for short bursts, which is as fast as an Olympic sprinter. When they reach their burrow, they dive in and use their wide behinds to block the entrance to keep the predator from following them.

Don't worry, predators can't chomp on a wombat's butt. Well, they can try. But wombats have super tough tushies made up of four fused bone plates covered in extra layers of **cartilage**, thick skin, and fur. This protective barrier is called a dermal shield. Wombats use their reinforced rumps as a barricade, shielding their more vulnerable body parts and any other wombats in the burrow. Even if the predator bites or claws them, it doesn't do much damage.

Extra Booty: Wombats also have tiny, barely there tails, so there's nothing for a predator to grab and use as a handle to pull a wombat from its burrow.

In addition to using their shield-like butts for defense, wombats also use their hardy hineys as weapons. If you've ever watched knights fight in a movie, you might have noticed they use their shields for more than stopping swords. They also use the shields as weapons, swinging them at enemies to injure them. Wombats do something similar when protecting their burrows. If a predator manages to push its head into the entrance, the wombat uses its strong legs to slam its butt against the predator's head. *Wham!* It crushes the predator's skull against the roof of the burrow, killing it. That's one deadly derrière!

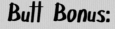

Butt Bonus:

WOMBAT POOP IS SHAPED LIKE CUBES! THE REASON FOR THE ODD-SHAPED DOODY IS THAT WOMBATS MARK THEIR TERRITORY BY POOPING ON ROCKS AND LOGS, AND THE SQUARE SHAPE STOPS THE PELLETS FROM ROLLING OFF ONTO THE GROUND. THEY PRODUCE 80 TO 100 CACA CUBES PER NIGHT TO TELL OTHER WOMBATS TO STAY AWAY.

What do you think about these buns of steel? How would you rate the wombat in the Battle of the Butts?

😛 TERRIFIC TUSHIE   😄 REMARKABLE RUMP   😎 COOL CABOOSE   😕 PASSABLE POSTERIOR   😒 BORING BACKSIDE

CHALLENGER

3

THE BUM
BREATHER

INTRODUCING

THE FITZROY RIVER TURTLE!

Species: *Rheodytes leukops*

Length: 10 inches (25 centimeters)

Weight: 4.4 to 5.5 pounds (2 to 2.5 kilograms)

Home Turf: The rivers and creeks of the Fitzroy Basin in Queensland, Australia

Posterior Power: They breathe through their butts.

Achoo! If you breathe through your butt, is that a sneeze or a fart? Okay, the Fitzroy River turtle does not actually inhale or exhale air through its rear end, so there won't be any sneeze-farts. In fact, the turtle's butt breathing is similar to the way a fish uses its **gills** to absorb oxygen from water.

As the first step of this rump respiration, the Fitzroy River turtle pumps water into its behind. The area then splits into two large sacs that are kind of like the turtle's butt lungs. However, these sacs are more like fish gills, with lots of blood vessels and surface area, which lets oxygen move from the water into the blood.

Extra Booty: Reptiles, birds, and amphibians have a single hole in their backsides that they use for peeing, pooping, and laying eggs, which is called the cloaca. So the technical term for the turtle's butt breathing is *cloacal respiration*.

The turtles still breathe air through their lungs, but by also absorbing oxygen through their butts, they can stay underwater longer. Even though several species of turtles can breathe through their butts, the Fitzroy River turtle is the champ. They absorb up to 70 percent of the oxygen they need through their booties. This means they can stay underwater longer than all the other turtles, for days or even weeks. The longest recorded time is three weeks!

Butt Bonus:

THE ONLY PLACE TO FIND THIS TURTLE IS NEAR THE FITZROY RIVER IN AUSTRALIA, WHICH IS HOW IT GOT ITS NAME. SINCE THEY'RE ONLY FOUND IN ONE AREA, AND THEY STAY UNDERWATER FOR SUCH LONG PERIODS OF TIME, SCIENTISTS DIDN'T DISCOVER THE FITZROY RIVER TURTLE UNTIL 1974. NOW THAT WE KNOW ABOUT THEM AND THEIR UNUSUAL WAY OF BREATHING, AUSTRALIANS HAVE GIVEN THEM THE NICKNAME BUM-BREATHERS.

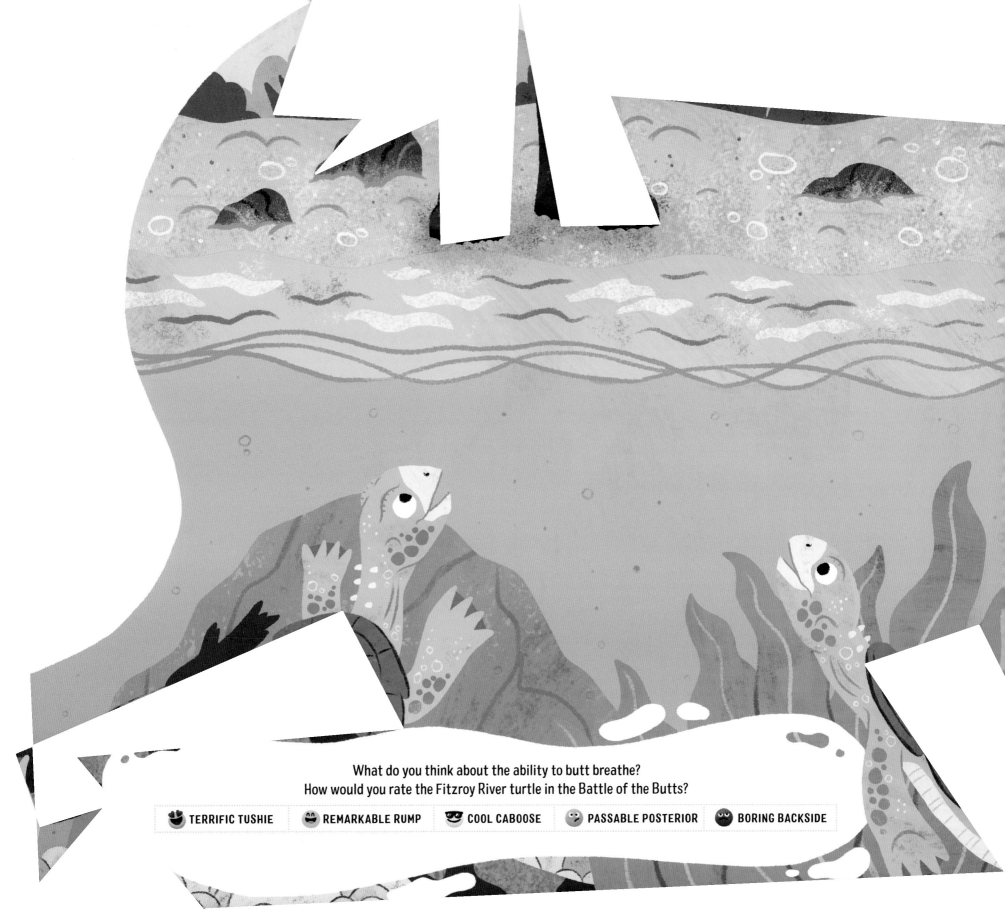

What do you think about the ability to butt breathe?
How would you rate the Fitzroy River turtle in the Battle of the Butts?

😀 TERRIFIC TUSHIE   😄 REMARKABLE RUMP   😎 COOL CABOOSE   😕 PASSABLE POSTERIOR   😑 BORING BACKSIDE

INTRODUCING

THE HERRING!

Genus: *Clupea*

Length: 8 to 15 inches (20 to 38 centimeters)

Weight: 7 to 10.5 ounces (200 to 300 grams)

Home Turf: The shallow, temperate waters of the North Pacific and North Atlantic oceans

Posterior Power: They communicate through farts.

Imagine your best friend is goofing off in class and doesn't see the teacher coming up behind them. You want to warn them, but you also don't want the teacher to *know* you're warning them. What if you could alert your friend with a fart? If you were a herring, you could! The small, silvery fish communicate with each other using their farts, which sound like high-pitched clicking noises.

Herring are social fish, and they stick together in huge groups called shoals. Shoals can contain millions of herring, and they help each other catch prey and avoid predators. To keep themselves organized in such a big group, they use the light reflecting off the silver scales of their nearby fish buddies to make sure they're in the correct position. But that only works during the day.

What do they do at night? They fart! Scientists noticed herring fart only after dark, so they believe the farts tell the other herring where they are to keep the shoal organized. Like "Bluuurp! Hey, dude, you're too close to my left, move over a few inches." Wouldn't you move over if your friend tooted next to you?

Herring have a great sense of hearing. They can hear **frequencies** much higher than we can, similar to the high frequencies dogs can hear. Their high-pitched farts are like a secret code their predators can't hear, so their fart-chats don't give away the location of the shoal.

Herring farts are not like our farts, though. We fart because of gases produced by the digestive process. Herring swallow air at the surface, which they store in their **swim bladders**. When they need to shout out to the other herring, they expel this air through their butts.

Extra Booty: The scientists who study herring farts named the sounds fast repetitive ticks or FRT for short.

Butt Bonus:

HERRING TOOTS ALMOST STARTED A WAR BETWEEN SWEDEN AND RUSSIA! THE SWEDISH MILITARY KEPT HEARING SOUNDS IN THE WATER LIKE THE POPPING AND HISSING OF FRYING BACON. THEY THOUGHT THE NOISES WERE BEING MADE BY RUSSIAN SUBMARINES TRESPASSING IN SWEDISH TERRITORY. THE LEADER OF SWEDEN SENT A LETTER TO THE LEADER OF RUSSIA DEMANDING THAT THEY REMOVE THEIR SUBMARINES FROM SWEDISH WATERS. THE RUSSIAN LEADER INSISTED THEY DIDN'T HAVE SUBS IN THE AREA. THINGS GOT VERY TENSE. FORTUNATELY, SCIENTISTS FIGURED OUT WHAT THE NOISES ACTUALLY WERE BEFORE THE TWO COUNTRIES STARTED FIGHTING OVER HERRING FARTS.

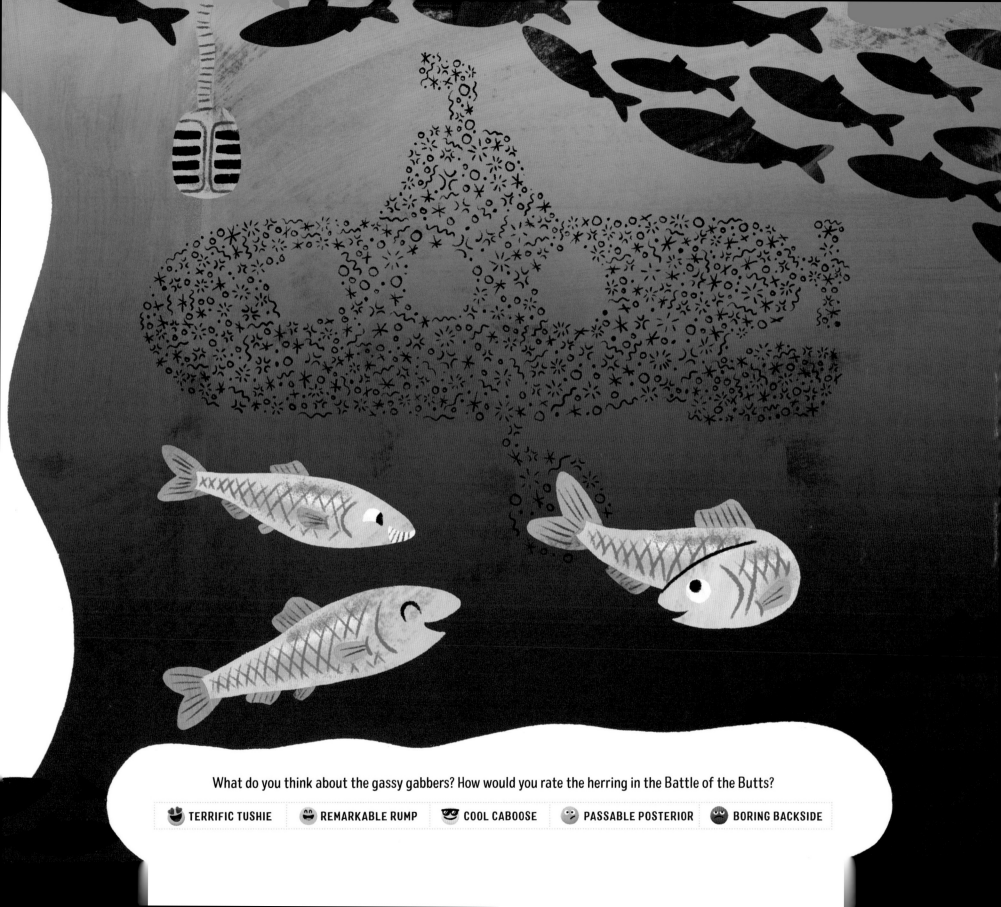

What do you think about the gassy gabbers? How would you rate the herring in the Battle of the Butts?

TERRIFIC TUSHIE | REMARKABLE RUMP | COOL CABOOSE | PASSABLE POSTERIOR | BORING BACKSIDE

CHALLENGER

✦5✦

THE CANNON
CABOOSE

INTRODUCING

THE BOMBARDIER BEETLE!

Family: *Carabidae*

Length: 0.0787 to 1.181 inches (2 to 30 millimeters)

Weight: 0.0045 to 0.015 ounces (0.128 to 0.424 grams)

Home Turf: The temperate woodlands and grasslands of all continents except Antarctica

Posterior Power: They shoot boiling chemicals out of their butts.

A bombardier beetle strolls through the leaves, minding its own business. A bunch of hungry ants attack. Things don't look so good for the beetle. Then . . . *Pew! Pew! Pew!* The bombardier beetle fires a pulsing spray of scalding chemicals from its butt, twisting its tushie in different directions to hit all the ants. The bombardier beetle escapes, while the ants regret their decision to snack on the beetle.

How do bombardier beetles turn their butts into super soakers filled with burning liquid? They store chemicals in separate areas in their hind ends. When they feel threatened, they mix the chemicals together, and an explosive reaction occurs. It's similar to the science fair project where vinegar and baking soda are poured into a model of a volcano to make lava erupt. Except the bombardier beetle's "lava" actually burns.

The bombardier beetle has two glands in its abdomen that open at the tip of its butt. Each gland has two chambers. The big chamber is the storage compartment for the fuel, which is a mixture of hydrogen peroxide (the same stuff your parents might use to clean cuts and scrapes) and another chemical called hydroquinone. The smaller chamber next to the tip is called the reaction chamber and has special **enzymes** in it that act like a match when they come in contact with the fuel. A **valve** separates the two chambers to keep them from mixing.

When the bombardier beetle feels threatened, it squeezes some of the fuel through the valve into the reaction chamber and *BOOM!* The chemicals mix together and all kinds of exciting things happen. First, they combine into new chemicals that irritate the eyes and respiratory system. Second, the liquid in the bombardier beetle's butt heats up to 212°F, which is the boiling point of water. Ouch! Finally, all of this mixing creates pressure, like shaking a soda can, and the burning mixture is forced out of the bombardier beetle's booty with an explosive pop you can hear.

This all happens very quickly, at an average rate of 500 pulses per second. The ejected liquid can reach a speed of 22 miles per hour. And bombardier beetles have excellent aim, which makes them even more dangerous. Their butts can swivel 270 degrees, which means they can shoot their burning spray at attackers coming from almost any direction. They can even rotate it upward to spray over their back at predators attacking from the front.

Extra Booty: It's a good thing bombardier beetles have such great aim, because they can only blast 20 times in a row before they run out of chemicals in their glands.

Butt Bonus:

IN MOST CASES, A BOMBARDIER BEETLE DEPLOYS ITS DEFENSES *BEFORE* IT GETS EATEN, BUT FROGS HAVE SUPER-FAST TONGUES. IF A BOMBARDIER BEETLE GETS SWALLOWED BY A FROG, IT SETS OFF ITS BUTT BOMB *INSIDE* THE FROG'S STOMACH. THIS OFTEN MAKES THE FROG BARF OUT THE BOMBARDIER BEETLE STILL ALIVE! JAPANESE SCIENTISTS RUNNING EXPERIMENTS ON FROGS EATING BOMBARDIER BEETLES COULD ACTUALLY HEAR THE TINY EXPLOSIONS IN THE FROGS' STOMACHS WHEN THE BOMBARDIER BEETLES' BUTTS DETONATED. IN 43 PERCENT OF THE CASES, THE FROGS VOMITED UP THE BEETLES BETWEEN 12 AND 107 MINUTES LATER. BOTH THE BOMBARDIER BEETLES AND THE FROGS WERE FINE AND WENT THEIR SEPARATE WAYS AFTER THEIR DISGUSTING ENCOUNTER.

What do you think about the super soaker butt? How would you rate the bombardier beetle in the Battle of the Butts?

😋 TERRIFIC TUSHIE | 😀 REMARKABLE RUMP | 😎 COOL CABOOSE | 😐 PASSABLE POSTERIOR | 😒 BORING BACKSIDE

CHALLENGER

6

THE PROJECTILE
POOPER

INTRODUCING

THE SILVER-SPOTTED SKIPPER CATERPILLAR!

Species: *Epargyreus clarus*

Length: 1.38 to 2 inches (3.5 to 5 centimeters)

Weight: 0.0176 to 0.03 ounces (0.5 to 0.85 grams)

Home Turf: The edges of forests, swamps, and brushy areas from southern Canada to Northern Mexico

Posterior Power: Their butts are poop catapults.

P icture yourself relaxing in a cozy blanket fort. To make it even better, the blankets are *also* tasty snacks, so you don't have to leave to eat. You could stay there forever! Except for one problem: you still have to poop. If you were a silver-spotted skipper caterpillar, you could just stick your butt out of the entrance and fire away. Skipper caterpillars can shoot their poop pellets up to 38 body lengths away. In one study, a 1.5-inch caterpillar launched a pellet 5 feet!

Extra Booty: The scientific term for insect poop is *frass*. For the skipper caterpillar, you could call it fast frass because the poop pellets (which are the size of Nerds® candy) travel at 4.3 feet per second.

How do these little guys manage to fling their frass so far? As they push out a pellet, the blood pressure in their butt increases. The pellet falls against a hinged plate in their butt, while pressure keeps building. When the pressure reaches its peak, it slams into the plate, which then smacks the pellet like a tennis racket. *Whack*—the poop pellet flies through the air.

The reason skipper caterpillars fling their frass is to keep predators from finding them. Before becoming butterflies, skipper caterpillars live in shelters they make from leaves. They make these "leaf forts" by folding down leaf edges and sticking them together with silk they spin. These leaf shelters hide them from predators who hunt by sight. Sometimes the skipper caterpillars come out to eat, but often they munch on the leaves of their shelter to stay hidden.

But some predators, especially wasps, hunt for skipper caterpillars by the smell of their frass. If skipper caterpillars were to stick their butts out of their leaf shelter and poop on their porch, the wasps would follow the smell of the poop right to their front door. By firing their frass several feet away, skipper caterpillars point the wasps in the wrong direction. They actually fling their frass in several different directions to further confuse the wasps by making sure a pile doesn't form in one place to give away their position.

Butt Bonus:

WHAT HAPPENS TO ALL THE FRASS THAT GETS FLUNG BY SKIPPER CATERPILLARS? ANTS USE IT FOR GROWING FOOD! THERE ARE MORE THAN 200 SPECIES OF ANTS KNOWN AS FUNGUS–GROWING ANTS. INSTEAD OF COLLECTING FOOD, THEY ARE TINY LITTLE FARMERS. THEY BRING NUTRIENTS BACK TO THEIR NESTS AND USE THEM TO GROW FUNGI TO FEED THEIR COLONIES. ONE OF THE NUTRIENTS USED TO GROW THEIR FUNGUS GARDEN IS CATERPILLAR POOP PELLETS.

What do you think about the ability to catapult caca?
How would you rate the silver-spotted skipper caterpillar in the Battle of the Butts?

😈 TERRIFIC TUSHIE 😀 REMARKABLE RUMP 😎 COOL CABOOSE 😕 PASSABLE POSTERIOR 😟 BORING BACKSIDE

CHALLENGER

7

THE FATAL
FARTER

INTRODUCING

THE
BEADED
LACEWING!

Species: *Lomamyia latipennis*

Length: 0.0484 to 0.161 inches (1.23 to 4.1 millimeters)

Weight: 0.0000024692 ounces (0.07 milligrams)

Home Turf: The temperate regions of North America

Posterior Power: Their farts are deadly.

Confession time. Have you ever farted on someone, like your sister, brother, or best friend? Sure, it's gross, but at least it's not dangerous like if a beaded lacewing did it because *their* farts kill!

Luckily, these poisonous poots only kill one creature—termites. While a beaded lacewing is in its **larval** stage, it lives in termite nests. When it feels hungry, the beaded lacewing larva approaches a termite and waves its butt in the termite's face. The termite is like, "Whatever, dude, that's rude," but it doesn't screech or run away like we do when someone farts on us. It doesn't react at all . . . at first. But after one to three minutes, the termite is flat on its back, paralyzed from the toxic toot.

The paralysis lasts three hours, giving the beaded lacewing plenty of time to snack on the termite. Beaded lacewings would make terrible party guests because, in addition to their fatal farts, they eat the same way spiders do. They have pointy mouths that are kind of like straws, which they use to inject digestive enzymes into the termites to turn their insides into liquid goo. Then the beaded lacewings slurp up the termite guts like a milkshake. Even if a beaded lacewing decides not to eat the termite after it lets loose its paralyzing poot, it's too late for the termite. At the end of the three hours of paralysis, the termite dies anyway.

Extra Booty: As beaded lacewing larvae get bigger, they can take out more termites with one toot—as many as six at a time!

Even though the beaded lacewing's gas is deadly to termites, it doesn't affect any other creatures. Scientists forced beaded lacewings to fart on other insects—like flies, wasps, and lice—but they were perfectly fine (other than being slightly offended).

So, what gives the beaded lacewing such fatal fumes? Scientists don't actually know. The researchers who originally studied the behavior of beaded lacewings didn't analyze the chemicals they produced, and there haven't been any other studies since then. Seems like it's time for a new round of research to figure out what makes beaded lacewing farts silent but deadly.

Butt Bonus:

IN ADDITION TO THEIR MYSTERIOUSLY FATAL FARTS, BEADED LACEWINGS HAVE ANOTHER ODD THING ABOUT THEIR DIGESTIVE SYSTEM—THEY DO NOT POOP UNTIL THEY TURN INTO ADULTS. WHILE THEY ARE LARVAE, THE INTESTINAL TRACT DOES NOT CONNECT ALL THE WAY THROUGH THE BODY. THE MIDGUT AND THE HINDGUT ARE SEPARATED, AND ALL THE WASTE COLLECTS IN THEIR MIDGUT. ONCE THEY **METAMORPHOSE** INTO THEIR ADULT FORM, THE GUTS FINALLY CONNECT, AND THEY ARE ABLE TO POOP FOR THE FIRST TIME. CAN YOU IMAGINE HAVING TO WAIT UNTIL YOUR EIGHTEENTH BIRTHDAY TO TAKE YOUR FIRST POOP?

What do you think about having a truly silent but deadly fart?
How would you rate the beaded lacewing in the Battle of the Butts?

TERRIFIC TUSHIE   REMARKABLE RUMP   COOL CABOOSE   PASSABLE POSTERIOR   BORING BACKSIDE

CHALLENGER

8

THE BEACH
BUM

INTRODUCING

THE PARROTFISH!

Family: Scaridae

Length: 1 to 4 feet (0.3 to 1.2 meters)

Weight: Up to 45 pounds (20 kilograms)

Home Turf: The shallow tropical
and subtropical waters around the world

Posterior Power: They build beaches with their butts.

Imagine yourself on a warm tropical beach surrounded by beautiful white sand. As the waves crash on the shore, you dig your toes into the soft, warm … poop! Yep, a large portion of that white sand is actually parrotfish poop. How do you feel about building a sand castle out of fish feces?

Extra Booty: Not all sand is made of parrotfish poop. Many beaches are formed by the weathering of rock and quartz. But if the white sandy beach is near a coral reef, like the beaches of Hawaii and the Caribbean, there's a good chance a parrotfish helped create it. It's estimated that some of the islands in the Maldives are 85 percent parrotfish doody.

This sandy surprise is due to the diet of parrotfish. Parrotfish eat the algae, **polyps**, and bacteria that live on and in coral reefs. Some species of parrotfish scrape the algae and bacteria off the coral, while other species actually bite off chunks of coral to get to the goodies inside. With all that scraping and chomping, parrotfish end up eating a lot of the coral's hard skeleton in addition to the food they actually want. Since their bodies can't use the coral skeleton, it gets ground up and pooped out as sand.

Chewing on coral is a lot like taking a bite out of a rock. If you were to try it, your teeth would break into pieces, but the parrotfish's goofy grin is serious business. They have about 1,000 teeth lined up in 15 rows, which are fused together to form a beak. Their teeth are made of fluorapatite, which is an extremely hard mineral. Parrotfish are a lot like sharks because when their teeth wear down from eating coral, they fall out and a new row is ready to replace it.

When you're snacking on coral, however, you need even more toothy power. So parrotfish have another set of teeth—in their throats! These throat-teeth work like a pepper grinder to crush the bits of coral into fine sand.

While parrotfish have tons of teeth, they don't actually have a stomach. After they grind up everything they have eaten, their meals go straight to their intestines. As the sandy mixture passes through the intestine, the nutrients from the algae, polyps, and bacteria are absorbed into the body. At the end of the journey through the intestine, beautiful white sand is pooped out, which people then play in without knowing its icky origin.

Butt Bonus:

PARROTFISH PRODUCE A WHOLE LOT OF SAND. THE SPECIFIC AMOUNT DEPENDS ON THE SIZE AND SPECIES OF THE PARROTFISH, BUT THE AVERAGE AMOUNT IS 200 POUNDS PER YEAR. THAT'S THE SAME AS POOPING OUT FOUR TENNIS BALLS EACH DAY. THERE'S A SPECIES OF HAWAIIAN PARROTFISH THAT PRODUCES 800 POUNDS OF SAND EACH YEAR. THAT'S LIKE POOPING OUT A HORSE PER YEAR!

What do you think about the ability to poop sand? How would you rate the parrotfish in the Battle of the Butts?

TERRIFIC TUSHIE   REMARKABLE RUMP   COOL CABOOSE   PASSABLE POSTERIOR   BORING BACKSIDE

CHALLENGER

9

THE TWO-HEADED
TOOTER

INTRODUCING

THE
SONORAN
CORALSNAKE!

Species: *Micruroides euryxanthus*

Length: 13 to 24 inches (33 to 61 centimeters)

Weight: 0.26 to 0.83 ounces (7.3 to 23.6 grams)

Home Turf: The rocky areas in Arizona, New Mexico, and western Mexico

Posterior Power: They fake out predators with their butts.

Sonoran coralsnakes are venomous, but they aren't really fans of biting. Instead, they use a few tricks to outsmart their predators. One of these tricks is to pretend its butt is its head!

Sonoran coralsnakes have the same red, yellow, and black bands as other coralsnakes in the United States. They have small, rounded heads that are about the same size as their blunt tails. Both their heads and the ends of their tails are black. They also have small eyes that blend into their heads. So basically, it's tough to tell their front end from their back end.

When threatened, a Sonoran coralsnake coils up and hides its head underneath its coils. Then it raises its tail and moves it around to make it seem like the tail is its head. If you're going to get chomped on by a predator, wouldn't you rather lose your tail than your head?

But that's not all! It also protects itself by farting. The Sonoran coralsnake sucks air into its butt and forces it back out to create farting sounds. Scientists have a few theories about why they do this. One, it might startle the predator enough to give the snake time to get away. Two, the farting sounds draw the predator's attention to the tail and away from the head buried in the coils.

Extra Booty: Since the Sonoran coralsnake is a reptile, just like the Fitzroy River turtle, it has a single hole in its backside called the cloaca used for peeing, pooping, and laying eggs. So the technical term for their farting sounds is *cloacal popping*.

These snake farts sound like high-pitched human farts, which is why some people call them microfarts. They've also been described as sounding like cloth ripping or blowing a raspberry. The pops come very quickly, each lasting less than two-tenths of a second. They can be heard up to six feet away. And since the snake is sucking in air to make the sound rather than using stored gas from digestion, it can repeat the popping multiple times.

Butt Bonus:

ANOTHER SNAKE THAT USES DEFENSIVE FARTING IS THE WESTERN HOOK-NOSED SNAKE. THEY LIVE IN THE SAME AREA AS THE SONORAN CORALSNAKES, SO SCIENTISTS THINK THE TWO SPECIES OF SNAKES MIGHT HAVE EVOLVED THIS FORCED FARTING TO WARD OFF A COMMON PREDATOR. WESTERN HOOK-NOSED SNAKES SEEM EVEN MORE ENTHUSIASTIC ABOUT THIS ABILITY THAN SONORAN CORALSNAKES; THEY HAVE BEEN SEEN BOUNCING OFF THE GROUND FROM THE ENERGY THEY PUT INTO THEIR FARTS.

What do you think about having a whoopee cushion for a butt?
How would you rate the Sonoran coralsnake in the Battle of the Butts?

😄 TERRIFIC TUSHIE   😁 REMARKABLE RUMP   😎 COOL CABOOSE   🤨 PASSABLE POSTERIOR   🙁 BORING BACKSIDE

INTRODUCING

THE SEA CUCUMBER!

Class: Holothuroidea

Length: 0.75 inches to 6.5 feet (2 centimeters to 2 meters)

Weight: 0.88 to 5.5 pounds (400 to 2500 grams)

Home Turf: The seafloor of oceans throughout the world

Posterior Power: Their butt is a Swiss Army knife of abilities.

It's tough to know where to start with sea cucumbers, because their butts do *so many* weird things.

Let's start with a familiar posterior power—breathing through the butt. Yep, there's more than one kind of animal that breathes through its behind! Like the Fitzroy River turtle, sea cucumbers pump water into their butts to get oxygen. Unlike the turtle, sea cucumbers always breathe this way because they don't have lungs. Instead, they have respiratory trees, which are tubes with lots of branches running along both sides of their bodies. Sea cucumbers use their butts to pull water into their respiratory trees, and then the oxygen from the water passes through the thin walls of the tubes into the cells of their bodies.

With all this water pumping through sea cucumber butts, scientists wondered what was happening to the **plankton** and other food particles. So they fed sea cucumbers **radioactive** algae to trace the food moving through their bodies. While it would have been cool if the radiation gave the sea cucumbers *super* powers, it was almost as cool to discover sea cucumbers have another *posterior* power—they eat through their butts! They enjoy most of their meals through their mouths, but any food that gets sucked in through their bums during breathing gets transferred from the respiratory tree to the intestine. Waste not, want not, right?

Extra Booty: Scientists looked at the sea cucumber's respiratory tree under a microscope and found small, finger-like projections called microvilli. They help absorb nutrients and are usually found in the intestine, so it was further proof sea cucumbers eat through their butts. In order to sound less gross, scientists decided to call this ability bipolar feeding.

Speaking of intestines, another posterior power of some sea cucumbers is shooting their guts out of their butts. They do this when threatened by a predator, and the type of organs sea cucumbers expel from their booties depends on their species. They eject parts of their intestines, respiratory trees, or reproductive organs in a process called evisceration. This distracts the predator and gives them something to munch on while the still-alive sea cucumber gets away. But don't worry, sea cucumbers can re-grow their organs! Depending on which organs were expelled, it can take from 7 to 145 days to replace them.

And if breathing, eating, and shooting organs out of their butts isn't weird enough, sea cucumbers have another posterior power—their butts are hotels for other animals. A few crabs and clams like living in the butts of sea cucumbers, but the most common resident is the long, skinny pearlfish. Pearlfish take advantage of the fact that sea cucumbers breathe through their butts, so when they open their anus to inhale or exhale, the pearlfish pushes itself inside its cozy new home.

Most species of pearlfish just use sea cucumbers for protection. They come out to eat and stay close to their mobile homes in case they need to escape a predator. But some species of pearlfish are actually **parasites**. They snack on the soft tissue *inside* the sea cucumbers. Rude! Luckily, sea cucumbers are able to **regenerate** the organs the pearlfish eat, but they probably still wish the pearlfish would find a new place to live.

Extra Booty: To make sea cucumber butts *even weirder*, some species have anal teeth. These are scary-looking spines around the opening of their bums. Scientists theorize they are there to keep out uninvited guests, but since some pearlfish slither past them anyway, experts aren't completely sure if they are defensive or not.

Butt Bonus:

SIMILAR TO PARROTFISH, SEA CUCUMBERS POOP OUT SAND. HOWEVER, THEY DON'T MAKE THE SAND LIKE PARROTFISH. INSTEAD, SEA CUCUMBERS END UP EATING A LOT OF SAND AS THEY SNACK ON ALGAE AND WASTE MATERIAL FROM THE SEAFLOOR. THEY DIGEST THE GOOD STUFF AND POOP OUT THE SAND MUCH CLEANER THAN IT WAS BEFORE. THEIR POOP HELPS CORAL REEFS, SEAGRASS, AND OTHER PLANTS, AND IMPROVES THE HEALTH OF THE ECOSYSTEM.

What do you think about having such a multipurpose butt?
How would you rate the sea cucumber in the Battle of the Butts?

😄 TERRIFIC TUSHIE   😀 REMARKABLE RUMP   😎 COOL CABOOSE   😕 PASSABLE POSTERIOR   😣 BORING BACKSIDE

AND THE WINNER IS . . . ?

Nature clearly has a sense of humor. Butts were already funny on their own, what with all the pooping and farting, but then nature decided to give some butts special talents. Butts used for breathing. Butts used for eating. Butts used for swimming. Butts used for talking. Butts used for defense. Butts that can build things. Butts that can kill.

But the question remains: who has the best buttocks of them all?

Here's a reminder of the challengers:

THE PUDGY POOTER A.K.A.
THE MANATEE

THE TOOT TALKER A.K.A.
THE HERRING

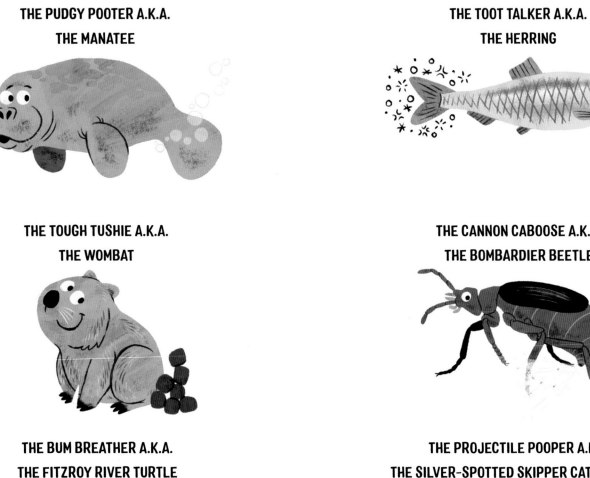

THE TOUGH TUSHIE A.K.A.
THE WOMBAT

THE CANNON CABOOSE A.K.A.
THE BOMBARDIER BEETLE

THE BUM BREATHER A.K.A.
THE FITZROY RIVER TURTLE

THE PROJECTILE POOPER A.K.A.
THE SILVER-SPOTTED SKIPPER CATERPILLAR

THE FATAL FARTER A.K.A.
THE BEADED LACEWING

THE TWO-HEADED TOOTER A.K.A.
THE SONORAN CORALSNAKE

THE BEACH BUM A.K.A.
THE PARROTFISH

THE HOTEL HINEY A.K.A.
THE SEA CUCUMBER

You rated them as you read, but now you have to pick a single winner.

Do you pick the most powerful butt? The most dangerous butt? The butt that can do multiple things?

Or maybe you pick the butt that makes you laugh the most.

It's up to you.

You now have the sacred duty of crowning the ultimate King of Keisters.

GLOSSARY

Buoyancy: the ability of an object to float or rise when in a liquid

Cartilage: a tough, elastic tissue stiffer than muscle but not as hard as bone (In humans, it's found in the ears, nose, and joints.)

Diaphragm: a sheet of muscle that separates the chest and the abdomen in mammals and helps control breathing

Enzyme: a protein that helps a chemical reaction take place within a living thing, such as the digestion of food

Frequency: the number of sound waves that pass a certain point each second, used to measure how low or high a sound is

Gill: organ used for breathing by fish and other water animals by absorbing oxygen from water

Larva: the wingless, worm-like version of an insect after it hatches from an egg but before it changes into an adult

Marsupial: a group of mammals in which the female has a pouch outside her belly to carry her young

Metamorphose: to change in form or transform, like a caterpillar into a butterfly

Parasite: an animal or plant that lives in or on another living thing and gets food or protection from it without giving anything in return

Plankton: a mixture of microscopic plants and animals floating in water

Polyp: a small water animal with a soft body that attaches itself to underwater objects

Posterior: a fancy name for butt

Radioactive: giving off rays of energy as a result of the decay of unstable atoms

Regenerate: to grow new tissue or parts to replace injured body parts

Swim bladder: a gas-filled sac in fish that regulates buoyancy

Valve: a flap that controls the flow of liquid in a body